W9-AOZ-265

OCT 1 2 2017

EXPLORE
my world

Ducklings

Marfé Ferguson Delano

NATIONAL
GEOGRAPHIC
KiDS

WASHINGTON, D.C.

It's a wood duck!

In early spring, she flies through a tangle of branches and lands by a hole high up in a tree.

What's in
the hole?
Her nest.
What's in
the nest?
Her eggs.

5

Day and night, the mother duck sits on the eggs to keep them warm. Inside the eggs, baby ducks are growing.

6

After about 30 days,
peck, peck, peck!
The baby ducks
are ready
to hatch.

Crack!

The baby ducks tap and peck and push their way out of their shells. They are wet and sticky and tired. Hatching is hard work!

The next morning, the mother duck leaves the nest and swims in the lake below the tree. She softly calls to her ducklings: *oo-oo-oo-ee, oo-oo-oo-ee.*

Tweep, tweep, the fuzzy ducklings cheep. They want to be with their mother, but they can't fly yet. So they climb to the edge of the hole in the tree and ...

Jump!

One by one, the ducklings leap from the tree. Down they go, tumbling and turning. Splash!

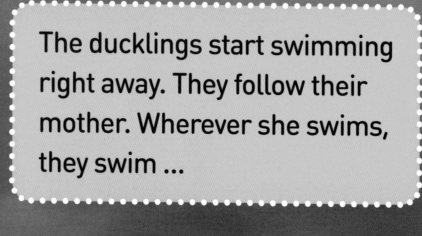

The ducklings start swimming right away. They follow their mother. Wherever she swims, they swim ...

... wherever she waddles, they waddle ...

... wherever she sits, they sit ...

... and wherever she sleeps, they sleep.

Yum!

When the ducklings get hungry, they dip their heads into the water and scoop up plants and bugs and other small animals in their beaks.

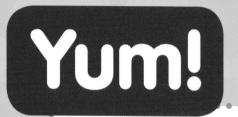

The ducklings grow up fast. When they are about two months old, they grow a new set of feathers. And with these new feathers, they learn to ...

Fly!

Now the ducklings are on their own. No more following Mom!

male

The ducklings keep growing and changing. By summer's end, the males are as colorful as a box of crayons. The females look like their mother.

female

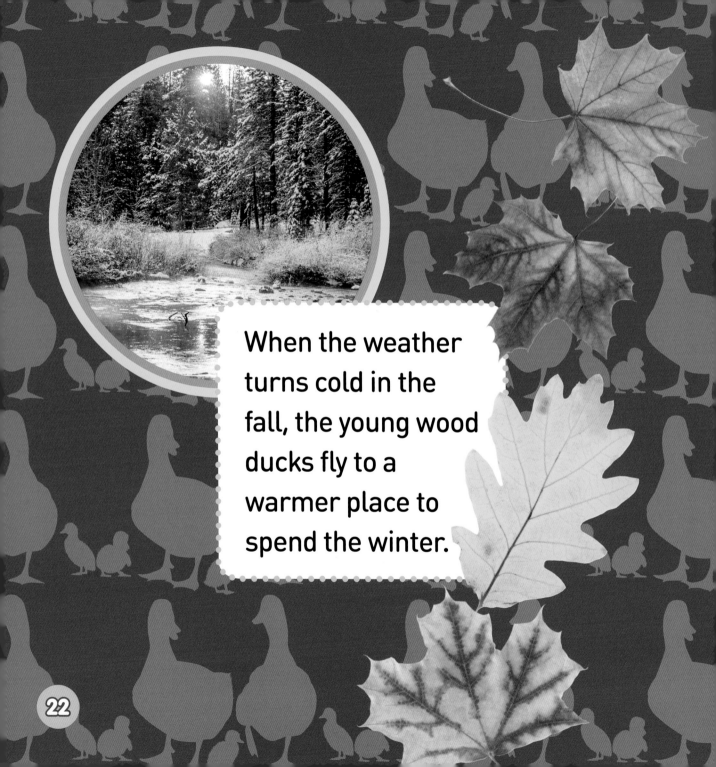

When the weather turns cold in the fall, the young wood ducks fly to a warmer place to spend the winter.

When spring comes, a male wood duck and a female wood duck will fly to the lake together. The female will lay her eggs in a tree hole nearby.

Follow me!

And one fine morning, the new mother duck will call for her ducklings to leave the nest and join her: *oo-oo-oo-ee, oo-oo-oo-ee.*

caterpillar

Egg-cellent Animals

lizard

Ducklings, ostrich chicks, owlets, and other baby birds all hatch from eggs laid by their mothers. But they aren't the only baby animals that come out of a shell. Here are some other "egg-samples."

grasshopper

sea turtle

tadpole

corn snake

alligator

Ducky Details

Wood ducks are built for climbing, perching, eating, walking, swimming, floating, and flying. Here are some of the features that help them do these things and more.

Wide, flat beak for scooping up food

male

Sharp claws on toes for climbing and perching on branches. Webbed feet are perfect for swimming, floating, and walking.

How many different colors can you count on the male duck? How many on the female duck?

Waterproof feathers keep ducks dry.

How do you keep dry?

female

Underneath their outer feathers, grown-up ducks have a layer of soft feathers called down. Ducklings are covered with down when they hatch. It helps keep them warm.

How do you keep warm?

A wide, rectangular tail helps wood ducks balance on tree branches.

29

Let's Be Ducklings!

1

Curl up in an egg shape. Curl, curl, curl!

2

Peck out of your shell. Peck, peck, peck!

3 Shake out your feathers. Shake, shake, shake!

4 Jump from the nest. Ready, set, *wheee!*

5 Splash down in the water. Splash, splash, splash!

6 Swim in the water. Paddle, paddle, paddle!

7 Go for a walk. Waddle, waddle, waddle!

8 Spread your little wings. Flap, flap, flap!

To my father, Forest Ferguson, with love and gratitude —MFD

Copyright © 2017 National Geographic Partners, LLC
Published by National Geographic Partners, LLC,
Washington, D.C. 20036

All rights reserved. Reproduction of the whole or any part of
the contents without written permission from the publisher
is prohibited.

Since 1888, the National Geographic Society has funded more than
12,000 research, exploration, and preservation projects around the
world. The Society receives funds from National Geographic Partners,
LLC, funded in part by your purchase. A portion of the proceeds from this
book supports this vital work. To learn more, visit www.natgeo.com/info.

NATIONAL GEOGRAPHIC and Yellow Border Design are trademarks of
the National Geographic Society, used under license.

Trade paperback ISBN: 978-1-4263-2715-5
Reinforced library binding ISBN: 978-1-4263-2716-2

The publisher gratefully acknowledges Dr. Gary Hepp, formerly of
Auburn University's School of Forestry and Wildlife Sciences, for his
expert review of the book.

Printed in Hong Kong
17/THK/1

ILLUSTRATIONS CREDITS

Front cover, Tammy Wolfe/Alamy; Back cover (LO), Russell
Burden/Getty Images; Throughout (Wave Patterns), Vector Draco/
Shutterstock; Throughout (Duck Patterns), weter 777/Shutter-
stock; Throughout (Duck Footprint Patterns), Wiktoria Pawlak/
Shutterstock; 1 (CTR), Stan Tekiela; 2–3 (CTR), rmarnold/Getty
Images; 4-5 (CTR), Lennie and Uschi Rue III/Rue Wildlife Photos; 6
(CTR), Rolf Nussbaumer Photography/Alamy Stock Photo; 7 (CTR),
Stan Tekiela; 7 (LO CTR), Dorling Kindersley/Getty Images; 8 (UP),
Dorling Kindersley/Getty Images; 8 (LO), Studio-Annika/Getty
Images; 9 (CTR), Steve and Dave Maslowski; 10 (CTR), Russell
Burden/Getty Images; 11 (LO), Steve Bloom Images/Alamy Stock
Photo; 13 (CTR), Nathan Lovas; 14-15 (CTR), Scott Leslie/Minden
Pictures; 15 (CTR), Mircea Costina/Alamy Stock Photo; 16-17
(CTR), Russell Burden/Getty Images; 18 (UP), Jelger Herder/
Minden Pictures; 18 (LO LE), Joel Sartore/National Geographic;
18 (LO RT), Ursula Rue; 19 (CTR), erniedecker/Getty Images; 20
(CTR), FotoRequest/Shutterstock; 21 (UP), Juan Aunion/Shut-
terstock; 21 (LO), FotoRequest/Shutterstock; 22 (UP), Robert
Yockey/EyeEm/Getty Images; 22 (RT), iStock.com; 22 (RT), Julia
Filipenko/Shutterstock; 23 (CTR), Steve Gettle/Minden Pictures;
24-25 (CTR), Russell Burden/Getty Images; 26 (UP), Eric Isselee/
Shutterstock; 26 (CTR), agust_syahrivana/Getty Images; 26 (LO),
Eric Isselee/Shutterstock; 27 (UP LE), Mark Conlin/VWPics/Alamy
Stock Photo; 27 (UP RT), Pete Oxford/Minden Pictures; 27 (CTR),
Life on white/Alamy Stock Photo; 27 (LO RT), Michel Gunther/
Minden Pictures; 28-29 (CTR), Danita Delimont/Getty Images; 28
(LO), LifetimeStock/Shutterstock; 29 (UP LE), Darrell Gulin/Getty
Images; 29 (UP RT), Ivan Kuzmin/Shutterstock; 29 (CTR), Colin
Carter Photography/Getty Images; 30 (UP), Russell Burden/Getty
Images; 30 (LE), Russell Burden/Getty Images; 30 (CTR), KidStock/
Getty Images; 30 (LO RT), Liquidlibrary/Getty Images; 30 (UP),
Russell Burden/Getty Images; 31 (UP LE), Westend61/Getty Imag-
es; 31 (UP CTR), David Tipling/Getty Images; 31 (UP RT), Thomas
Barwick/Getty Images; 31 (LO LE), DOUGBERRY/Getty Images; 31
(LO CTR), Hero Images/Getty Images; 31 (LO RT), Martin Puddy/
Getty Images